MW01093420

GENOCIDE IN MODERN TIMES™

# THE KHMER ROUGE AND THE CAMBODIAN GENOCIDE

Sean Bergin

ROSEN
PUBLISHING®

New York

Published in 2009 by The Rosen Publishing Group, Inc.
29 East 21st Street, New York, NY 10010

**Library of Congress Cataloging-in-Publication Data**

Bergin, Sean, 1968–
The Khmer Rouge and the Cambodian genocide / Sean Bergin. — 1st ed.
    p. cm.—(Genocide in modern times)
Includes bibliographical references and index.
ISBN-13: 978-1-4042-1822-2 (library binding)
1. Cambodia—Politics and government—20th century. 2. Cambodia—Politics and government—1979– 3. Genocide—Cambodia. 4. Pol Pot.
5. Parti communiste du Kampuchea. I. Title.
DS554.8.B473 2009
959.604'2—dc22

2008000004

*Manufactured in the United States of America*

**On the cover:** Background: Photographs of the victims of the "Killing Fields" are displayed at the Tuol Sleng Museum of Genocidal Crimes in Phnom Penh. Foreground: Cambodian Buddhist monks ride with the body of the former Khmer Rouge leader Ta Mok.

# CONTENTS

# INTRODUCTION

The word "genocide," first coined in 1944, literally means the murder of an entire group or class of people. The term was formally defined by the United Nations (UN) in 1948, following the extermination of millions of Jews, Gypsies, Catholics, homosexuals, and others by Nazi Germany during World War II (1939–1945). Hoping to prevent future similar instances of horrific, state-sponsored mass murder, the UN drafted the Convention on the Prevention and Punishment of the Crime of Genocide. According to the UN convention, genocide was any act, committed during war- or peacetime, designed to destroy a national, ethnic, racial, or religious group, either through murder, infliction of severe mental and physical suffering, interference with reproduction, or other means of removing children from the targeted group. The UN General Assembly adopted it on December 9, 1948, thereby binding all member nations to

These piles of killed Cambodians' skulls and bones are a horrific reminder of the murderous reign of Pol Pot, the leader primarily responsible for the Cambodian genocide of 1975–1979.

observe the new international law and punish its violation by private individuals, public officials, or national rulers.

Although the Holocaust was the first widely recognized genocide, genocide was by no means new to the twentieth century. Tribal, nationalist, ethnic, and religious groups have warred against each other since the earliest days of recorded history. Periodically they engaged in slaughter of each other's innocent civilian populations. Yet, the technological advances of the twentieth century made it possible to exterminate human life in unprecedented numbers and with alarming speed. Machine guns, automatic weapons, tanks, bombs, chemical and biological weapons, flamethrowers, and other forms of industrialized weaponry made it possible to eliminate whole villages, towns, and cities in a matter of days, if not hours.

The century opened with the Turkish genocide against the Armenians, a still disputed and poorly understood atrocity that became overshadowed by the Holocaust. The century limped to its conclusion with both the Serbian "ethnic cleansing" of Bosnian Muslims and Croats in the wake of the disintegration of the former Yugoslavian state and the tribal genocide in Rwanda perpetrated by Hutus against Tutsis. And there is no indication that genocide will subside anytime soon. The first years of the twenty-first century have already been soiled by the murder of about half a million Darfurians in Sudan by government-sponsored militias and death squads. As many as 2.5 million more have been displaced, their villages and crops destroyed. Women and children are routinely raped. Survivors' lives in refugee camps are precarious and dangerous.

Despite the adoption of the UN Convention on Genocide, the global community has not always been able to prevent or punish mass murder of entire groups of people. Sometimes, it has not even been willing or able to notice or acknowledge genocide when it occurs or bring its perpetrators to justice once the facts finally surface. Such is the case with one of the twentieth century's most appalling but still relatively unexamined instances of genocide in Cambodia. Almost two million

Cambodians (about one-fifth of the population) were killed through execution, starvation, torture, and exhaustion under the Khmer Rouge Communist regime led by the militant dictator Pol Pot.

Pol Pot instituted an astonishingly ruthless and violent reorganization of Cambodian society. He was a Khmer, Cambodia's dominant ethnic group accounting for about 80 percent of the population. Seeking to both purge the nation of foreign influence and non-Khmer ethnic "taints" and impose a radical Communist agrarian system, Pol Pot persecuted ethnic Vietnamese, Thai, and Chinese Cambodians. He evacuated cities, relocated urban dwellers and intellectuals to the country, and forced them into backbreaking agricultural labor. Setting up the simple Khmer peasant as the national ideal, he and his Khmer Rouge comrades executed intellectuals, killed anyone unable to adapt to the forced labor, and exterminated ethnic and religious minorities. In the end, he also murdered hundreds of thousands of ethnic Khmers. For this reason, a new term was created to describe his murderousness: autogenocide, the mass murder of one's own people.

Today, Pol Pot is dead, never having stood a real trial. He never spent a single day in prison paying for his unimaginable crimes. Members of his inner circle have also escaped justice to this point, though trials are pending. Cambodia is groping toward democracy but remains mired in poverty. And out in the countryside ravaged by Pol Pot—the so-called "Killing Fields"—the bones of almost two million people can be found lying exposed, in piles upon the ground.

# 1

## Cambodia's Long Road to Independence

Cambodia's golden age occurred between the ninth and fifteenth centuries, during the Angkorean empire, also known as the Khmer empire or the Kambuja kingdom. Centered in what is now northwestern Cambodia, the empire spread to include parts of modern-day Laos, Thailand, and Vietnam. The capital of the empire was the Angkor region, and this is where its kings lived. The region is believed to have been the world's largest preindustrial city, covering more than 100 square miles (259 square kilometers) and containing several million residents.

Yet, the Angkorean empire began to fall into decline as Thai forces began to harass the region. By the mid-fifteenth century, the Thai kingdom of Ayutthaya had seized the capital region. Within a short period of time, the ever-encroaching jungle reclaimed Angkor, shrouding it in a dense tangle of creeping greenery.

### THE FRENCH COLONIAL PERIOD

What followed was four hundred years of repeated attacks, invasions, and domination by both Vietnam and Thailand. In 1863, the Cambodian king Norodom, who had been installed by Thai overlords, requested French protection. France had established

The Angkor Wat temple complex has been reclaimed from the jungle that once shrouded it and is now an enormously popular tourist destination.

colonial outposts in neighboring parts of Southeast Asia and promptly accepted Norodom's invitation to administer what it called Cambodge. In English, this was translated as both Kampuchea and Cambodia (all of these names referred to the Kambuja kingdom of Cambodia's golden age).

France was beginning to build a powerful series of colonies throughout Southeast Asia, known collectively as French Indochina. It included Cambodia, Laos, and Vietnam. Cambodia's new "protector" quickly began to seize control of its rice, corn, fish, timber, and rubber plantations, as well as its tobacco, silk, and cotton textile industries. France exported these natural resources and products, taxed both the peasants who harvested them and the merchants who exported them, and collected the profits.

France also took charge of Cambodia's foreign affairs, economy, and defense. The French provided the government, bureaucracy, language, and armed forces. They imported Vietnamese to fill civil-service positions and provide skilled labor. Merchants and shopkeepers were often Chinese. Most Cambodians merely existed, it would seem, to labor in the fields, provide agricultural exports for France, pay taxes to their colonial masters, and suffer from malnutrition and hunger. It was as if they were guest workers in their own country. Even King Norodom was given no real power other than as a symbolic figurehead.

French colonists seek shelter from the hot sun and steamy air in Indochina in 1900.

While Cambodian unrest and outright revolts were few and far between during the French colonial period, France's colonies in Vietnam were experiencing similar hardships, and their resentment did begin to boil over into rebellion. This took the form of a series of assassinations of colonial officials and large-scale peasant revolts. Most troubling, from the French perspective, was the formation of the Indochinese Communist Party (ICP), in 1930. Though dominated by Vietnamese leadership, the ICP began to attract growing numbers of Cambodians who were belatedly beginning to feel stirrings of nationalist fervor and anticolonial resentment.

With the outbreak of World War II in 1939, France was overrun by Germany. The French authorities in Cambodia were now too distracted, isolated, and overwhelmed to properly attend to Cambodia's interests. Germany had granted its ally Japan effective control over Indochina. In turn, Japan allowed the French to retain token control over most of Cambodia, but real power and authority had shifted to the Japanese. The French colonial rulers, long accustomed to setting up puppet Cambodian kings, had become puppets themselves.

## GROWING CAMBODIAN NATIONALISM AND INDEPENDENCE

In 1941, during World War II, the French chose Prince Norodom Sihanouk to succeed his grandfather, King Monivong. As the war began to draw to its bloody close, France was liberated from Nazi Germany's occupation by Allied troops, and its colonial officials once again began to exert control over Indochina. The kingdoms had changed in their absence, however. The brief taste of semi-independence from France during World War II had reignited the nationalist spark for many Cambodians. Pride mingled with shame as Cambodians contemplated how far their culture had fallen and how subservient and dependent

King Norodom Sihanouk reviews troops as part of a ceremony during his visit to Paris, France, in June 1946, soon after the French reasserted colonial control over Cambodia.

they had become. They became determined to halt this slide into dependence and victimization and began to greatly mistrust and resent foreign interference in their affairs.

All of these crosscurrents combined to sweep away French colonial rule over Cambodia. Communist guerrillas in northern Vietnam known

Vietnamese soldiers rest between assaults during the 1954 battle of Dien Bien Phu, in which French forces were defeated. This loss led to the collapse of French colonial rule throughout Indochina.

as the Viet Minh had led the resistance to Japanese forces during the war and stoked nationalist fervor. Following Japan's surrender, they began agitating against renewed French rule, as did some nationalist Khmer forces. By 1953, King Sihanouk had converted to the rapidly growing Cambodian independence movement and began to campaign for the withdrawal of the French. The next year, following a devastating loss at the hands of the Viet Minh in the battle of Dien Bien Phu in Vietnam, France granted Cambodian independence. Norodom Sihanouk was now the undisputed leader of a sovereign nation. His satisfaction at this turn of events would be short-lived, however, as Cambodia was about to be torn apart by a Communist-inspired civil war.

It was during this chaotic time that Saloth Sar renamed himself Pol Pot and first entered the roiling stream of historic events. In him was crystallized the weight of Cambodians' the tragic history and their blossoming hatred—for the French, for all foreign interference, for ineffective and self-serving royalty, for their Vietnamese and Thai neighbors, and for all things non-Khmer and untraditional. Yet, concentrated in this one strange and charismatic man, the collective rage of an entire nation would prove impossible to control or contain. All of Cambodia would become its ultimate victim.

# 2

## The Boy Who Would Become Pol Pot

The seemingly happy, peaceful, and unremarkable child who would grow up to become Pol Pot was probably born in March 1925, though unreliable French colonial records indicate May 25, 1928. He was born to two ethnic Khmer parents who named him Saloth Sar. His father, Phen Saloth, was a fairly successful farmer in the village of Prek Sbauv, 90 miles (145 km) north of Cambodia's capital, Phnom Penh. Phen Saloth owned 50 acres (20.23 hectares) of rice paddy and gardens, as well as buffalo and cattle. He was wealthy enough to build a tile-roofed house, the largest in the village.

### ELITE BUT MEDIOCRE

Saloth Sar's family was prosperous, and he was spared working in the fields. He never knew hunger or hard labor, and he received a good education. Through several family members, he even had useful connections to the Royal Palace in Phnom Penh. These connections allowed Saloth Sar to leave his humble village behind, travel to Phnom Penh, and attend a Buddhist monastery favored by the royal court. After a year there, he began attending an elite Catholic primary school, the Ecole Miche. Its teachers were French and Vietnamese, and lessons were given in French. This kind of

A Cambodian farmer plows his rice field with the help of oxen. More than 80 percent of Cambodians are farmers, and rice is the nation's primary crop and export product.

education was usually reserved for French nationals and aristocratic Cambodians. Most ordinary Cambodians received no primary education at all.

During the time Saloth Sar studied at the Ecole Miche (1937–1942) and the equally elite secondary school College Sihanouk (1942–1947), he seemed to have made little impression on his fellow students. He was remembered as a bland, quiet, polite boy who was average in every way and a mediocre, unmotivated student. In 1948, he failed a crucial exam that would have admitted him to the upper classes of the Lycée

A young Saloth Sar rests in a Cambodian field. As Pol Pot, he and the Khmer Rouge would orchestrate and oversee the murder of millions of his own people in fields like this one across the nation.

Sisowath, a select secondary school that would graduate many of Cambodia's future Communist leaders. Rather than continuing his studies with his far more accomplished and ambitious classmates, Saloth Sar enrolled in a technical school just outside Phnom Penh. There, he studied carpentry, widely regarded by faculty and students as the easiest of the school's subjects.

Though in many respects this turn of events could be considered a humiliation for a former member of the privileged class, Saloth Sar actually began to thrive at the technical school. His new efforts paid off almost immediately. In 1949, he studied for and passed an exam that earned him a scholarship to study radio electronics at an engineering school in France. Quite suddenly, Saloth Sar had reentered the elite, becoming one of only about two hundred Cambodians ever to be sent overseas for education and training.

## A PARISIAN AWAKENING

Saloth Sar arrived in Paris on October 1, 1949. It was a city enthralled by Communism, the strongest French political party of the time. Saloth Sar's political awareness was stimulated and nurtured by his friendships with

## A Face in the Crowd

At College Norodom Sihanouk, the high school that Saloth Sar attended in the city of Kompong Cham, the future Pol Pot made little impression on most of his classmates. David P. Chandler, author of *Brother Number One: A Political Biography of Pol Pot*, spoke to several of Saloth Sar's classmates:

"His manner was straightforward, pleasant, and very polite," one of them said. Another recalled that Sar "thought a lot, but said very little," while a third noted that he spent much of his spare time playing basketball and soccer: "He was a pretty good player, but not outstanding." Saloth Sar seemed to have no clear ambitions. He was content to drift along, enjoying his companions without making a strong impression on them, secure in the knowledge that he was among friends ...

fellow Cambodian students who had become Communists. In his second year of study in Paris, he began attending political debates and discussions hosted by these friends. Some participants remember Saloth Sar as being an exceptionally articulate and passionate leader of these discussions, while others can barely remember his presence, which they say was sporadic.

Regardless of his true level of involvement in these student gatherings, by 1952, Saloth Sar had become a member of the Communist Party of France. In response to a growing combined Communist and pro-democracy movement in Cambodia, King Norodom Sihanouk dissolved the National Assembly, arrested members of opposition political parties, and declared martial law. Communists, nationalists, and the Cambodian students in Paris were all outraged and motivated to action.

The Paris headquarters of the French Communist Party flies a banner adorned with symbols of Communism and portraits of Vladimir Lenin *(left)* and Joseph Stalin in 1952, the year Saloth Sar joined the party.

Indeed, even Saloth Sar, ordinarily so passive and reluctant to apply himself or stand out, was inspired to get actively involved in the Communist struggle to "liberate" Cambodia.

Having failed out of school and lost his scholarship, Saloth Sar could not stay in Paris much longer. He returned to Phnom Penh in January 1953, just as King Norodom Sihanouk was trying to stave off nationalist and Communist rebellion by personally urging the French to grant Cambodia its independence.

Once back in Cambodia, Saloth Sar quickly met up with Viet Minh forces of the Indochinese Communist Party (ICP) entrenched near the Vietnamese border. The ICP was aggressively recruiting Cambodians to form all-Khmer guerrilla units and militias. By late 1953, the ICP controlled about one-third of Cambodian territory and as much as one-half of its population. Its sister organization, the Khmer People's Revolutionary Party (KPRP), was also growing rapidly with ICP sponsorship and successfully recruiting Cambodian peasants and former Buddhist monks.

# INDEPENDENCE AND A LULL BEFORE THE STORM

As a member of the French Communist Party, Saloth Sar was accepted into the ICP. The Communist forces escalated their rebellion, and soon France accepted the fact that it could no longer hold onto Indochina without prolonged war, great loss of life, and diminishing economic value. At the Geneva Conference of 1954, France relinquished all claims to Indochina. To quell fighting, it was decided that Vietnam would be

Viet Minh forces march triumphantly through the streets of Hanoi, North Vietnam, following the signing of the Geneva accord in 1954. The accord granted the Communists control over the northern half of Vietnam.

divided into two halves—a Communist north and non-Communist south—until national elections could be held. Viet Minh forces in the southern half of Vietnam could either disarm or relocate to the north. In Cambodia, nationalist and Communist forces were expected to disarm, but many Khmer Communists instead went into exile in North Vietnam.

King Sihanouk hoped that his strong fight for independence from France and his ensuing declaration of Cambodian international neutrality would dampen any further armed rebellion against his rule. Sihanouk stuck to his word and resisted American efforts to gain influence in Cambodia. The United States was intent on fighting Communism throughout the world. Nationalists and Communists in Cambodia were bent on resisting American involvement, which to them was a new form of colonialism, dressed up as Cold War politics.

Average Cambodians, including many Democrats, gradually made their peace with Sihanouk's rule, and he actually began to enjoy widespread popularity. The KPRP and ICP lost much of their momentum, no longer able to harness widespread Cambodian anger and recruit Khmer fighters. Many Khmer Communists decided they had achieved the most important goals of Cambodian independence and simply returned to their ordinary lives.

Even Saloth Sar appeared to reenter conventional life, marrying a woman named Khieu Ponnary and becoming a schoolteacher at a private college in Phnom Penh. He was by all accounts a warm, gentle, encouraging, and supportive instructor. Yet, at the very same time, Saloth Sar began to use his revolutionary pseudonym "Pol." He was working actively with the ICP to build a bigger and better Cambodian Communist Party, drawing mainly on the urban elite, including students, teachers, and Buddhist monks. Like many other urban-elite Khmer Communists, Saloth Sar had not given up the fight. He had merely gone underground and was biding his time.

# 3

## The Emergence of the Khmer Rouge

By 1960, North Vietnamese Communists were staging attacks in South Vietnam against the American-backed government there. They were also seeking to enlist the help of Laotian and Cambodian Communists in their struggle. To this end, they sponsored a party conference in which the Revolutionary Workers' Party of Kampuchea was formed. It would later change its name to the Communist Party of Kampuchea and often be referred to simply as the Cambodian Communist Party. Norodom Sihanouk called them the Red Khmers, or, in French, the Khmer Rouge. Though this was meant to look like an autonomous, independent party, it initially received nearly all of its direction and supervision from North Vietnam.

### UNDER THE THUMB OF THE VIETNAMESE

In 1962, Saloth Sar became acting secretary of the party's Central Committee while still leading his respectable life as a married schoolteacher in Phnom Penh. Following an especially harsh police crackdown against the Cambodian Communist Party, however, Saloth Sar opted to leave Phnom Penh, abandoning his "cover" as a schoolteacher to flee to eastern Cambodia. Once there, he began working in a Vietnamese military camp at the border of Cambodia and Vietnam.

For the next seven years, Saloth Sar and his fellow Cambodian Communist militants lived in remote corners of eastern and northeastern Cambodia, shuttling between rebel camps, and existing under the thumb of Vietnamese Communists. The North Vietnamese kept their Cambodian counterparts unarmed. The only weapons they had were those they were able to capture from Sihanouk's forces. Unable to wage armed warfare, and restricted in their movements by their Vietnamese masters, the Cambodian Communists mostly served as scouts, guards, laborers, and "gofers."

## AMERICAN BOMBING AND A STRANGE NEW ALLIANCE

Meanwhile, American involvement in the growing war in Vietnam was escalating, first with military observers and then fighting soldiers deployed in ever-increasing numbers. As Vietnamese Communists began to take shelter more often in Cambodia, American bombing raids along the Vietnam-Cambodia border became more frequent. Cambodian civilian casualties were high. Rural Cambodians were outraged and blamed Sihanouk, believing that the bombing was occurring with his blessing. The ranks of Cambodian Communist members swelled dramatically, and armed rebellion increased. The country was dissolving into chaos as both a Cambodian civil war and a Vietnam-American war were being waged on Cambodian territory simultaneously. The chief of Sihanouk's police force, Lon Nol, sensed impending disaster. Seeing a political opportunity as well, he conspired against his boss and removed Sihanouk from power in a bloodless coup in March 1970.

Always a wily and opportunistic political operator, Sihanouk, in exile in China, forged an alliance of convenience with his former Communist enemies. Together he, his loyalists, and the Cambodian Communists would form the National Liberation Front, allied with Vietnamese Communists and trained and supplied by Vietnamese armed forces. The goal was to

Troops patrol the smoldering ruins of a Cambodian shopping center following an American bombing in 1970.

overthrow the treacherous and harshly repressive Lon Nol, who was almost universally despised by Cambodians of every background.

Saloth Sar reemerged from the shadows to assume military leadership of this new alliance. As chief of the military directorate of the National Liberation Front, Saloth Sar gladly accepted Vietnamese training and weaponry. Looking toward the future, however, he sought to create a more self-sufficient corps of Khmer fighters who would not be indebted to or dependent upon Vietnamese masters. He began recruiting, educating, and training young Phnom Penh residents, mostly of the intellectual classes

Lon Nol, former general under Norodom Sihanouk, appears in this April 1970 photograph, one month after he overthrew Cambodia's royal leader in a bloodless coup. He went on to name himself prime minister and ruled the nation with an iron fist until the Khmer Rouge takeover in 1975.

(teachers, students, and degree-holding professionals).

Yet, over time, he began to hold up the ideal of the Cambodian peasant and laborer. He came to insist that Khmer Communist Party members should be drawn from these ranks, rather than from an intellectual class often "tainted" by associations with privilege, European elitism, and the monarchy. His goal was to establish a new society based upon Communist principles of communal ownership of land, collective work, and the nobility of the peasant and laborer. He intended to demolish the class system, mainly by forcibly converting or destroying members of the upper classes to which he himself belonged and owed his success.

## THE KHMER ROUGE GOES IT ALONE

With Vietnamese training, arms, direction, and manpower, the rebellion against Lon Nol went well. As a result, the increasingly Communist-dominated National Liberation Front gained control over much of the rural territory throughout Cambodia. Lon Nol's forces shrank back and hunkered down in Phnom Penh and other cities. Saloth Sar seized the opportunity offered by this relative calm to preach Communist revolution throughout the nation, recruit among peasants and workers, and force the people of the villages he controlled to adopt his social and political policies.

The United States began to believe that the Vietnam War was not winnable and that the former Indochina was probably lost to Communism. It decided to remove troops as quickly as it could and negotiated a cease-fire with North Vietnam. The Khmer Rouge refused to stop fighting in Cambodia, however. It felt outraged and betrayed that Vietnam, having achieved its goals in its own country, was now so

In this 1971 photograph, a U.S. tank crew expresses its wishes to return home and leave the fight against Communist North Vietnam to America's South Vietnamese allies. The United States would remain in Vietnam for another four years.

A wounded Cambodian government soldier is carried away by comrades following a violent skirmish with Khmer Rouge rebels in 1973.

willing to abandon the fight for Communist victory in Cambodia. Saloth Sar decided the Khmer Rouge would fight on, alone if necessary.

With no cease-fire in place in Cambodia, the United States took parting shots at the Communist enemy by again heavily bombing Cambodia. Some two million Cambodian refugees fled the firestorm, their homes, villages, and farms destroyed. Once the bombing ceased, in less than six months, the Khmer Rouge gained large numbers of new recruits, traumatized and embittered by the American bombing. The Khmer Rouge had swelled from a ragtag force of about three thousand men in 1970 to about sixty thousand men and women by 1973. It had also become far better armed and better trained. Saloth Sar decided that at long last the time was right to emerge from the countryside to swarm Phnom Penh and seize the seat of government.

## THE FALL OF PHNOM PENH

The Khmer Rouge's newly effective and dangerous fighting force launched a series of attacks upon Phnom Penh from 1973 to 1975. The first two assaults were beaten back by Lon Nol's army. In late 1974, however, Saloth Sar's Khmer guerrillas surrounded Phnom Penh, seized the roads leading into and out of it, and mined the Mekong River. Then they

Khmer Rouge soldiers march into Phnom Penh following Pol Pot's seizure of the Cambodian capital on April 17, 1975, after a siege lasting more than three months.

began an artillery bombardment of Phnom Penh. Lon Nol fled the city and went into exile. On April 17, 1975, Khmer Rouge troops marched into the capital to a joyous welcome.

Most residents of Phnom Penh believed that the Khmer Rouge victory would mark the end of war, the restoration of Sihanouk, and the return of peace and stability. Yet, Norodom Sihanouk was now Cambodia's leader in name only. He was forcibly sidelined and kept in exile by Saloth Sar, who named himself "Comrade Secretary" and appointed twelve other men and women as various ministers and cabinet secretaries. These were the true leaders of a nation rechristened Democratic Kampuchea (DK), a country with a new name that was about to be radically transformed. Even the flow of Cambodian history was to be redirected, as Saloth Sar proclaimed it to be "Year Zero" for Democratic Kampuchea.

The Phnom Penh residents who were in the streets celebrating the Khmer Rouge victory did not know that Saloth Sar had already crafted a plan for what to do with the "enemies" of his Communist movement, nor did they know that *they* were now considered party enemies. Any residents of urban areas formerly controlled by Lon Nol who had not left their cities to join the Khmer Rouge were now viewed as traitors.

During the siege of Phnom Penh, Saloth Sar decided that these enemies would be forcibly removed from the cities, marched into the countryside, and put to work. Khmer Rouge propaganda claimed that this would be ennobling work for these corrupt intellectuals and capitalists. It would make them good Khmer peasants. In reality, however, Saloth Sar, who soon began referring to himself as Pol Pot, was about to transform the Cambodian countryside into a massive forced-labor camp, political prison, and execution chamber. The cheering crowds who greeted Khmer Rouge troops that day in April could not possibly conceive of the deadly nightmare that was about to be visited upon them.

# 4

# The Cambodian Genocide

Cambodia's urban residents who had not migrated to the country-side to join the Khmer Rouge in the time leading up to Pol Pot's victory suddenly became a new class of people. Whether ethnically Khmer or not, they were now contemptuously referred to as "new people" and "April 17 people." They were not like the "old people," the Khmer peasants and workers who had fought and triumphed over the French, Americans, and monarchy. Instead, in the eyes of Khmer Rouge militants, they had lived a life of luxury while the "original Khmers" were being bombed, displaced, and killed in revolutionary battle.

## EVACUATION AND RELOCATION

Following the Khmer Rouge victory, the two million residents of Phnom Penh were told that an American bombing campaign was about to begin, and that, for their safety, they must evacuate the city for two or three days. Many were robbed of the possessions they took with them, and their houses were looted. Goods that were thought of as elitist were particularly forbidden, such as wristwatches, jewelry, electronics, cars, motorcycles, and foreign currency. It was claimed that the party needed these items to

After Khmer Rouge forces seize Phnom Penh, its residents stream out of the city on April 17, 1975. Carrying as many of their possessions as possible, they are unknowingly headed to the "Killing Fields" of the Cambodian countryside.

help further the aims of the revolution and build up Democratic Kampuchea.

Bonfires were set to burn books, especially Buddhist teachings and French-language texts. Those who refused to leave their homes or part with their belongings were threatened with violence, beaten, and often shot. The evacuees were assured that the officials and armed forces of Democratic Kampuchea would look after their well-being. Yet, as many as twenty thousand people died from hunger or exhaustion or were executed during the forced march to the countryside.

Upon reaching the rural villages to which they were assigned, each urban evacuee was required to write a brief autobiography, focusing on family background, youth and education, and profession. Most important, he or she had to account for his or her time during the Lon Nol regime. Each evacuee's immediate fate was decided by the content of his or her essay. Those with a background in the military, government, "elite" Western professions like engineering and architecture, and education (including schoolteachers and university students), or who had had foreign contact of any kind were sent away for "reeducation." This usually meant they were executed. Sometimes, however, reeducation meant being sent to labor camps where starvation, torture, and interrogations were the daily routine. Skilled laborers often were sent back to the cities to get factories running again following the disruption of the Khmer Rouge takeover and the forced exodus of the urban population.

## POL POT'S AGENDA

Pol Pot's goal for Democratic Kampuchea was to achieve total self-sufficiency within four years. Pol Pot wanted to destroy Cambodia's traditional agricultural model of peasants laboring for a monarch or an urban elite. Instead, every Cambodian would now become a peasant and labor for the party and the nation, for the common good.

Laboring for the nation meant building up the country and defending it against its historic enemies—France, Vietnam, and the United States. More generally, it meant defending it from weakness, dependency, and need. If Cambodia's agricultural industry could develop enough so that it could adequately feed the nation and provide trade income, then Cambodia would be able to beef up its industries. Never again, Pol Pot declared, would Cambodia be dependent upon other nations for anything it needed, including self-defense.

In order to throw all their effort and focus behind agricultural output, the vast majority of Cambodians would be relocated to cooperative farms

Cambodian peasants thresh wheat in an agrarian labor camp in 1978. The Khmer Rouge leaders banned all modern technology in order to purify the Cambodian people.

and villages (which were basically labor camps). Private property and religion would be banned. Banking, money, and markets would be abolished and replaced with a barter system. Though its members were almost all European-educated, the DK leadership prized illiteracy and de-emphasized education. It also treated high culture—including art, literature, dance, music, and Buddhist art and teachings—with hostile contempt. Hospitals, schools, and factories were closed. Buddhist monks were stripped of their robes and forced to labor in the rice fields. Families were intentionally separated, with infants removed from parents as soon as they were finished breast-feeding. It was believed that this would help ensure that people viewed the DK as their family and work hard for it, rather than for personal goals. All sentiment, attachment, and passion would now be directed to Democratic Kampuchea.

The director of the Cambodian National Library in Phnom Penh sorts through debris following a Khmer Rouge attack in December 1979.

## LIFE AND DEATH IN THE KILLING FIELDS

In this crazed push to move Democratic Kampuchea forward, millions of Cambodians suddenly found themselves laboring to clear forests, create and irrigate rice fields, build dams, and plant and harvest rice. Every element of their lives was controlled by cadres, or officials, of the village cooperative to which they had been assigned.

The cadres were backed up by soldiers who were often only in their teens. Illiterate, uneducated sons and daughters of rural peasants, many of these youths had been traumatized by a childhood of civil war and American bombings. Their fear and anger were harnessed by Pol Pot, who also filled them with class and racial hatred for those "tainted" by non-Khmer traits, such as the possession of higher education, a foreign language, or minority ethnicity. Cadres and their soldiers understood that while the DK leadership was not troubled by excessive violence, it was enraged by leniency toward perceived enemies. Therefore, they frequently erred on the side of murderous repression, if only to save their own lives.

Under strict commands from DK's leadership, rice yields were expected to triple. In order to meet these obligatory targets, local commanders overworked the laborers. They worked fourteen- to eighteen-hour days, were fed a few tablespoons of watery rice a day, and lived in heavily guarded labor camps. "Old people"—the peasants who lived in the rural areas held by Communists before the fall of the Lon Nol regime—were given more and better rations and better living quarters. They were also allowed to join the army, the party, and their village's governing committee. "New people"—city dwellers evacuated to the countryside following Pol Pot's victory—were fed less, were punished more, had no rights, and were much more likely to be executed.

Death rates among "new people" were far higher than those of "old people." In many villages, rice harvests were too small to adequately feed all the new arrivals. Malaria and leeches were common, and on any given day as many as half of a village's workers could be idled by sickness. Only those who worked a full day received their ration of rice. Missing one's daily production goals meant receiving less food, more work, or both. Hunger and disease became a vicious downward spiral. Sometimes, disease and incapacity were viewed as anti-party rebelliousness, and the ill person was executed as an enemy of Democratic Kampuchea.

Yet, as time went on, unrealistic harvest goals were not met, hunger increased, and the "old people" began to suffer mistreatment and deprivation nearly as much as the "new people." Starving peasants foraged for lizards, snails, crabs, spiders, and wild vegetables. A cooperative village might suffer three or four dozen deaths a day. Gravediggers were reported to be dropping dead while burying the dead. Those who made mistakes, missed their production goals, were too ill to work, or accidentally

# Cambodian Children Tell Their Stories

Pol Pot was so successful in creating a closed society and in isolating Cambodia from the rest of the world that news of the ongoing genocide rarely leaked beyond the nation's borders. The world gradually became aware of the Khmer Rouge atrocities following the eventual Vietnamese defeat of Pol Pot in 1979, as survivors' stories became known. Dith Pran, himself a survivor of Khmer Rouge death camps and the inspiration for the important 1984 film *The Killing Fields*, collected many Cambodian children's stories.

**Seath K. Teng, aged four at the time of the Khmer Rouge takeover:** "The Khmer Rouge soldiers told us not to love our parents or to depend on them because they are not the ones who supported us. They told us to love the new leaders and to work hard so that our country could be prosperous. If we didn't do as they said, we would get a severe beating for punishment . . . [T]hey made us cheer and keep repeating that we love, work hard for, and respect our new government . . . [B]efore sunlight, they shouted and whistled for us to get up and get in line to go to work."

**Gen L. Lee, aged seven at the time of the Khmer Rouge takeover:** "All I knew for over three years was that hunger and death were forever present. All I cared about was food, and sometimes I did not want to live. Rations of food were meager . . . It was difficult to work more than ten hours a day on an empty stomach. I ate creatures and wild fruits and vegetables that I would not have eaten during better times. I was not good at catching field rats and frogs. Snails, crabs, and tiny fish were easier to catch and hide."

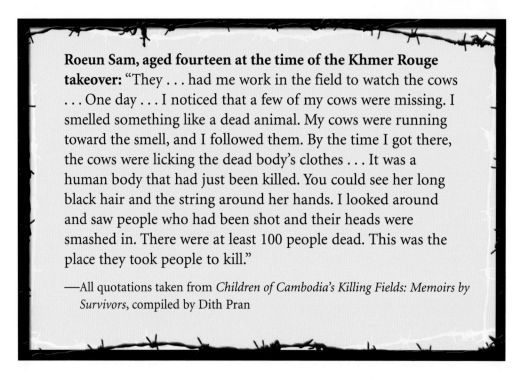

Roeun Sam, aged fourteen at the time of the Khmer Rouge takeover: "They . . . had me work in the field to watch the cows . . . One day . . . I noticed that a few of my cows were missing. I smelled something like a dead animal. My cows were running toward the smell, and I followed them. By the time I got there, the cows were licking the dead body's clothes . . . It was a human body that had just been killed. You could see her long black hair and the string around her hands. I looked around and saw people who had been shot and their heads were smashed in. There were at least 100 people dead. This was the place they took people to kill."

—All quotations taken from *Children of Cambodia's Killing Fields: Memoirs by Survivors*, compiled by Dith Pran

broke farm equipment were often executed by electrocution, beheading, or butchering of the body.

Within three years of Pol Pot's reorganization of Cambodian society, hundreds of thousands of Cambodians were dying from starvation, malnutrition, overwork, poor or nonexistent medical care, and execution in the so-called Killing Fields. In order to conserve bullets, people were often beaten to death with farm implements, like axes, shovels, hoes, and spades. The clothes of those who died were removed from the bodies and given to others to wear. If not buried in shallow mass graves, corpses were left in fields to fertilize the soil, or they were burned in order to extract fertilizing phosphate from the bones' ashes.

## THE TUOL SLENG PRISON

The suffering and death were not limited to the countryside. Though Phnom Penh was largely emptied, one sector of it was still humming with activity. The Tuol Sleng interrogation facility, housed in a former school, was often the final destination for anyone Pol Pot deemed an enemy of Democratic Kampuchea. Also known as S-21, this facility was essentially a torture chamber and execution hall, ruled by the commandant Kaing

This scene of torture in Tuol Sleng prison was painted by the Cambodian artist Vann Nath, who was himself imprisoned, tortured, and nearly killed by the Khmer Rouge. His artistic talent saved him, and he was forced to paint celebratory portraits of Pol Pot. He is one of only six or seven survivors of Tuol Sleng.

Geuk Eav, known as "Duch." More than fourteen thousand people were brought to S-21. Only about six or seven people are believed to have survived their interrogation and imprisonment.

The prisoners were isolated, forced to be silent, shackled to the floor, hosed down in large groups only every few days, and fed a handful of watery rice every day. They became malnourished and sick, and many died before, during, or after interrogation. Torture tactics included electric shocks, cigarette burns, hanging upside down, forced ingestion of urine or feces, having fingernails pulled out, water immersion, suffocation, and beatings with sticks and electric wire.

Initially, the prisoners were military and government personnel associated with Lon Nol's administration. As Pol Pot became more and more paranoid, the definition of "enemy" was broadened to include any Cambodian who had studied abroad (just as Pol Pot and most of the DK leadership had) or had any contact with foreigners, Khmer Rouge deserters, and ethnic Khmers who had been living in Vietnam, including Khmer Communists trained and educated by the Viet Minh. These were considered "external" enemies, people who were in direct opposition to the DK's Communist agenda. Those who were viewed as "pollutants" to the purity of the Khmer were also killed, including homosexuals; ethnic Vietnamese, Chinese, Thais, and Laotians; tribal minorities; and Buddhists, Christians, and Muslims. Even those who wore eyeglasses (which were taken as a sign of dangerous intellectualism or elitism) were killed.

Later in his increasingly erratic and desperate rule, the "enemies" became internal. Pol Pot began to imagine himself surrounded by would-be traitors who were actually party members in good standing, some of them quite high ranking. Dragged in on charges ranging from poor agricultural production and sabotage to rebellious conspiracies and assassination attempts (probably more imagined than real), these Communist Party prisoners, like all the others at S-21, were interrogated, tortured, forced to write and sign phony confessions, and then executed. Bodies were buried in a cemetery on the property or in nearby fields.

The remains of executed Tuol Sleng prisoners are on display in the Killing Field known as Cheung Ek, outside Phnom Penh.

In the end, at least 1.7 million Cambodians—ethnic Khmers and ethnic minorities, "old people" and "new people," Communists and non-Communists, men, women, and children—died during Pol Pot's reign. About 200,000 of these were executions; the rest were due to torture, starvation, overwork, and related disease. Though his reign of terror lasted less than five years, one-fifth of the country's population was decimated.

Due to the extremely closed society Pol Pot had created, the world was mostly unaware that any of this devastation was occurring. Pol Pot would soon be swept from power, but he would escape justice and live hidden for many years in the country he all but destroyed.

# 5

## A Madman Unravels, a Nation Heals

Almost immediately after gaining power, Pol Pot sought to purge the nation of all Vietnamese influence. He killed those Khmers who had lived and trained in Vietnam, and he attacked the small Vietnamese minority living in Cambodia. He engaged in a number of border raids upon Vietnamese territory, including the heavy shelling of villages. Vietnam responded in kind, and these mutual attacks grew in frequency and intensity.

## VIETNAMESE INVASION AND THE DEFEAT OF THE KHMER ROUGE

As Cambodia continued to pester Vietnam at its borders, ethnic Cambodians in southern Vietnam grew rebellious. Vietnam decided to nip this growing problem in the bud. Beginning in late 1977, Vietnam began deeper invasions of Cambodian territory, capturing both prisoners and towns and cities. After withdrawing, Vietnam offered peace negotiations, but Pol Pot went on a rampage instead, shelling border towns, burning villages, and slaughtering Vietnamese civilians. Tit-for-tat attacks continued until Christmas Day 1979, when Vietnam launched a massive invasion of Cambodia, involving heavy artillery, tanks, fighter jets, and helicopters.

In a photo probably taken in Cambodia in the late 1970s, Pol Pot *(left)* stands next to Ieng Sary *(center)*, Pol Pot's foreign minister and friend from his student years in Paris.

Within two weeks, Vietnam forces reached Phnom Penh. Pol Pot's worst fears had come true, even if he had been the one to provoke the nightmare. The ancient adversary Vietnam was in firm control of his nation, and enemies now surrounded him. Pol Pot fled by helicopter and embarked on an eleven-year exile. Unrepentant and unbowed, he would continue to fight from a remote corner of the nation he once ruled and terrorized and live to escape punishment for his crimes.

As Vietnamese forces swept in, Khmer Rouge cadres and soldiers scattered. Many of them were killed in the fighting or died of disease and malnutrition as they hid in malaria-infested forests. Since the invasion halted the rice harvest, the long years of famine only worsened for Cambodia's beleaguered population, and thousands more died.

**41**

Khmer Rouge soldiers ride "war elephants" through the jungle of western Cambodia in 1981. Overthrown by Vietnamese forces in 1979, the Khmer Rouge would continue to wage civil war in Cambodia for almost twenty more years.

Vietnam set up a Communist puppet government, called the People's Republic of Kampuchea (PRK). It was mainly run by Khmer Communists who had fled to Vietnam before or during the Pol Pot reign and had not been Khmer Rouge members. Within two years, the Vietnamese had reintroduced money, markets, schools, hospitals, Buddhist practices, and family farming (as opposed to collective, cooperative farming).

## U.S. SUPPORT FOR POL POT

Still smarting from its defeat in Vietnam, the United States refused to recognize the PRK and instead supported Pol Pot and his still numerous Khmer Rouge troops, who were mostly exiled in Thailand. It did so despite the stories of Pol Pot's Cambodian genocide, which were finally beginning to be told to the outside world. The Khmer Rouge also received assistance from China, which was angered over Vietnam's close association with the Soviet Union, and Thailand, which feared a similar Vietnamese invasion.

The PRK put Pol Pot on trial in absentia (without his presence) and sentenced him to death, but Thailand declined to hand him over, and the United States refused to pressure it to do so. Once again, Pol Pot, despite his claims of independence and self-reliance, had benefited from the patronage of more powerful masters who were exploiting him for their own purposes.

Instead of forcing Pol Pot to face justice, the United States formed and sponsored a government-in-exile led by a dysfunctional coalition of former Democratic Kampuchea officials (and, therefore, high-ranking Khmer Rouge leaders), Norodom Sihanouk (who was living in China), and a former non-Communist Cambodian prime minister named Son Sann. The United States, China, and Thailand all offered this government financial assistance, and China provided its forces with arms.

Most of the coalition government's forces were Khmer Rouge. They were unable to recapture any significant portion of Cambodian territory, but the funding and weaponry allowed them to continue to wage war

## Through a Lens Darkly

In 1980, the Tuol Sleng prison was transformed into a museum, now called the Tuol Sleng Museum of Genocidal Crimes. In addition to its archive of four thousand coerced confessions and documents describing the prison's torture and interrogation practices and the daily life of prisoners and employees, the museum also houses hundreds of photographs of Tuol Sleng victims. Upon admittance to the prison, each prisoner was carefully posed and photographed. These are the final records of their last moments on earth.

*Cambodian Buddhist monks regard the skulls of executed prisoners on display at the Tuol Sleng Museum of Genocidal Crimes, formerly the site of the most notorious and bloody Khmer Rouge prison and torture chamber.*

> The prison's chief photographer, Nhem En, has been called before the tribunal trying former Khmer Rouge officials for war crimes. He will testify against Nuon Chea, believed to be the architect of the Khmer Rouge imprisonment and execution policies, and Kaing Guek Eav ("Duch"), the prison's commandant. Nhem En described his experiences to Seth Mydans, a *New York Times* reporter, in October 2007: "They [prisoners] came in blindfolded, and I had to untie the cloth . . . I was alone in the room, so I am the one they saw. They would say, 'Why was I brought here? What am I accused of? What did I do wrong?'"

and evade punishment for humanitarian crimes for another two decades. It also allowed the Khmer Rouge to heavily mine western Cambodia, resulting in the death or maiming of thousands of more Cambodians throughout the 1980s and 1990s. Traumatized Cambodians continued to live in terror of Pol Pot's possible return to power.

## POL POT'S UNRAVELING

By 1989, Vietnam had wearied of the Cambodian situation and withdrawn its troops. In 1991, an interim government to be supervised by the United Nations was agreed upon. Free elections to choose a new national government were scheduled, and all factions in the ongoing Cambodian war were to be disarmed. Pol Pot and the Khmer Rouge, however, refused to either disarm or participate in elections. The Royalist Party won the elections, returning King Norodom Sihanouk to the throne, though the position was purely ceremonial now. The Royalists entered into a coalition government with a party of former PRK officials. They soon declared the Khmer Rouge an illegal organization.

Joyous Cambodians cheer Vietnamese troops as the soldiers depart from the Cambodian city of Battambang in 1989. The withdrawal took place as Vietnam's decade-long rule over the country came to an end.

From its stronghold in western Cambodia along the Thai border, the Khmer Rouge continued to launch attacks, particularly against Vietnamese populations still in Cambodia. Pol Pot seemed to be descending into new depths of paranoia and madness. He ordered the execution of several of his leading and most loyal cadres, including his old friend and security chief, Son Sen, and Sen's wife and children. Mass defections from the Khmer Rouge began, including another of Pol Pot's oldest friends, Ieng Sary, a Parisian colleague and his former foreign minister.

Other leading Khmer Rouge cadres, fearing they would be executed next, decided to denounce and arrest Pol Pot. In July 1997, he was charged with treason by these leaders and put on trial in their jungle hideout. Most people felt this was a "show trial," designed only to improve the standing of the Khmer Rouge in international circles. If they could offer up Pol Pot for sacrifice, maybe they themselves would be spared punishment by Cambodian courts or international human rights tribunals.

A frail and ailing Pol Pot was sentenced to house arrest. He would die ten months later, unrepentant. In a series of interviews with journalist Nate Thayer that appear in David Chandler's book *Brother Number One,* he insisted his conscience was clear, even though he "did some things against the people." On April 15, 1998, Pol Pot passed away under armed guard. The Khmer Rouge effectively died with him.

Cambodians reacted with a bewildered combination of relief, joy, anger, and wary disbelief. "I don't want to believe that he's dead, and I don't have time in my life to believe Khmer Rouge propaganda anymore," Youk Chang, director of the Documentation Center of Cambodia, an organization that has collected genocide evidence for eventual use at a hoped-for human rights tribunal, commented to Keith B. Richburg of the *Washington Post*. Chang, a former political prisoner of the Khmer Rouge, went on: "If he's dead, hand over his body to the people, don't just take photographs. I want to see him handcuffed and pushed into a jail, like his cadres did to me twenty years ago."

Pol Pot speaks to a reporter while living under house arrest in his jungle hideout in northwestern Cambodia. This picture was taken about three months before his death.

Pol Pot died convinced that everything he did, he did for Cambodia and its people, and that there would no longer even be a Cambodia had he not risen to power. Pol Pot was a product of privilege, foreign education, and Vietnamese training. He set out to murder people who shared this very same background. In addition to these "new people" he exterminated and the members of ethnic minorities he ordered slaughtered, however, Pol Pot also destroyed the very Khmers he held up as an ideal—the uneducated Cambodian peasant. His radical reorganization of Cambodian society spun out of control as he began to imagine enemies everywhere he looked. His utopian vision curdled into genocide and autogenocide.

## CAMBODIA TODAY

Today, thanks to international aid, Cambodia is slowly beginning to rebound economically, though it is still burdened by political corruption. Norodom Sihanouk's son, Norodom Sihamoni, is now the ceremonial king, but Cambodia is a multiparty democracy with a prime minister and a Parliament.

The population is currently overwhelmingly youthful. The great majority of Cambodians were born after the Khmer Rouge genocide, and the national sense of trauma is beginning to gradually heal. This

## At Long Last, A Reckoning with the Past

In the summer and fall of 2007, five leading officials of the Khmer Rouge were arrested by Cambodian authorities and imprisoned. The five former members of Pol Pot's inner circle were Khieu Samphan, the Khmer Rouge president and Pol Pot's "Brother Number Two"; Nuon Chea, Pol Pot's right-hand man and mastermind of the Khmer Rouge's prison and execution policies and practices; Kaing Guek Eav ("Duch"), the commandant of the Tuol Sleng prison; Ieng Sary, the Khmer Rouge foreign minister and Parisian colleague of Pol Pot; and his wife, Ieng Thirith, social affairs minister and sister of Pol Pot's wife. They all have been charged with war crimes relating to the Cambodian genocide and will be tried by a tribunal established by the United Nations that includes both Cambodian and international judges.

In the past, Ieng Sary distanced himself from a decision-making role in the Khmer Rouge genocide. In a November 13, 2007, *New York Times* article, Sary was quoted as saying in 1996, "Pol Pot made all decisions on all matters by himself . . . [Pol Pot] killed people without careful consideration." Similarly, Duch has pointed the finger at Nuon Chea for the atrocities committed in Tuol Sleng. For his part, Nuon Chea shrugs off any responsibility and seems prepared to meet his fate calmly: "I will read books in prison, learn another language, and exercise. I will do all of this so that I can make myself strong. I told my wife not to visit me in jail and, if I die, not to make a ceremony but keep the money for my children's education. When I die, it will all be finished."

process has been helped along by the formation of a special court that was created with assistance from the United Nations to bring the surviving Khmer Rouge leadership to justice. This tribunal, to be led by three Cambodian and two foreign judges, may be able to finally administer

A young Cambodian boy and his sister take part in a march through Phnom Penh celebrating the fifty-ninth anniversary of International Human Rights Day. The December 2007 march was led by the UN special envoy for human rights and the U.S. ambassador to Cambodia, both of whom were demanding greater social justice for citizens of the impoverished nation.

some justice to those Khmer Rouge leaders most responsible for the national bloodletting.

Pol Pot, however, will remain forever beyond justice. The world mourns for the almost two million Cambodians he and his henchmen killed, but the only sentence passed upon him was his nation's utter joy at his death. In this sense, history has passed its harshest judgment upon the man who became Pol Pot.

# TIMELINE

**1925** Saloth Sar is born.

**1930** The Indochina Communist Party (ICP) is founded and dominated by Vietnamese membership and leadership.

**1937** Saloth Sar enters the Ecole Miche, an elite Catholic school in Phnom Penh.

**1940** France is conquered by Germany in the opening years of World War II. Germany offers control of Indochina to its Axis ally Japan.

**1942** Saloth Sar enters College Sihanouk.

**1945** World War II ends with Germany and Japan's surrender. France regains colonial control of Cambodia after a brief period of quasi-independence.

**1946** France grants limited political and constitutional freedoms to Cambodia. French troops battle ICP forces in northern Vietnam.

**1947–1949** Saloth Sar graduates from College Sihanouk, fails a university entrance exam, attends technical college, and receives a radio-electricity engineering scholarship for study in Paris, France.

**1951** The ICP encourages and sponsors the formation of the Khmer People's Revolutionary Party (KPRP), a supposedly independent Khmer Communist group that is in fact dominated by Vietnamese Communists.

**1952** Saloth Sar joins the French Communist Party and loses his scholarship. In Cambodia, King Norodom Sihanouk cracks down on Communists, declares martial law, dissolves the National Assembly, and rules by decree.

**1953–1954** Saloth Sar returns to Cambodia and joins up with the ICP. The French grant Cambodia independence. Khmer Communists take up residence in North Vietnam.

**1956** Saloth Sar, now married, becomes a schoolteacher but continues to work and recruit for the ICP.

**1960** The Worker's Party of Kampuchea (WPK) is formed, and Saloth Sar is on its Central Committee. The name will later change to the Communist Party of Kampuchea (CPK). Sihanouk refers to these Khmer Communists as "Red Khmers," or *Khmer Rouge*.

**1963** Saloth Sar goes into hiding and lives in a series of Communist Vietnamese military camps along the Cambodia-Vietnam border.

**1970** Sihanouk is overthrown in a bloodless coup, and his former police chief, Lon Nol, rises to power. Sihanouk forms a United Front government with Communist forces to seek Lon Nol's defeat and his own return to the throne. Saloth Sar becomes the chief of the front's military directorate.

**1971–1972** Khmer Rouge forces receive training and arms from Vietnamese Communists and strengthen greatly as a fighting force.

**1975** Khmer Rouge forces invade Phnom Penh and topple Lon Nol. Cambodia is renamed Democratic Kampuchea (DK). Saloth Sar emerges as the leader of DK and refers to himself as Pol Pot. The countries cities are evacuated, their residents forced to march into the countryside to be resettled in forced agricultural labor camps. Tens of thousands are executed or die during the march.

**1979** Repeated Khmer Rouge border attacks against Vietnam and Vietnamese populations in Cambodia prompt a Vietnamese invasion. Phnom Penh is captured, a Vietnamese-controlled Cambodian puppet government is established, and Pol Pot escapes into exile in Thailand.

**1973** The Khmer Rouge refuses a cease-fire agreed to by the United States and Vietnam. The United States heavily bombs the Cambodian countryside, resulting in thousands of new recruits for the Khmer Communists.

**1975–1979** Genocide against ethnic and religious minorities, foreigners, intellectuals, ethnic Khmers, and others deemed to be "enemies" of DK is carried out. Almost two million Cambodians die through overwork, disease, hunger, torture, or execution in prisons and agricultural labor camps.

**1989–1993** Vietnam withdraws its armed forces from Cambodia. A UN-supervised provisional government rules Cambodia until elections can be held. The Khmer Rouge refuse to disarm. The Royalists win the election, Norodom Sihanouk returns as king, though the country's governing power now rests with the prime minister and parliament.

**1994–1997** The Khmer Rouge continues to launch small-scale attacks and mine western Cambodia. Pol Pot begins to execute leading and longtime Khmer Rouge officials. Mass defections from the Khmer Rouge begin. Remaining Khmer Rouge leaders arrest Pol Pot, put him on trial for treason, and sentence him to house arrest.

**1998** Pol Pot dies.

**2007** Five leading members of the Khmer Rouge are arrested, charged with war crimes and crimes against humanity, and await trial by a Cambodian and international tribunal.

# GLOSSARY

**agrarian**  Relating to agriculture, or ownership, division, and management of land.

**atrocity**  An act of brutality and cruelty.

**autonomy**  The ability to be self-governing.

**Buddhism**  An Asian religion based upon the teachings of the sixth century BCE Indian philosopher Siddhartha Gautama.

**bureaucracy**  Managing of a government through a series of offices, departments, and agencies led by appointed officials and staffed by civil servants.

**collective**  Working together as a group; something that is worked on and achieved as a group.

**colony**  A body of people living in a new territory that is governed by a parent state.

**Communism**  An economic theory or system based upon the belief of community ownership of all property; the belief in a classless society, to be achieved by revolution if necessary, in which all goods are shared equally, and the state plans all aspects of the national economy.

**cooperative**  The owning of something by a group of members who share equally in the benefits and profits.

**corruption**  A loss of integrity or moral values; acting improperly or illegally in order to gain something.

**coup**  Short for coup d'etat, a term describing the violent overthrow or alteration of an existing government by a group of rebels.

**decimate**  To destroy.

**elite**  The most distinguished, powerful, or well-regarded group.

**empire**  A political entity that encompasses a large territory or group of territories and includes many different peoples, all united under a single, overarching governing structure.

**exile**  A period of enforced or voluntary absence from one's home.

**famine**  A severe shortage of food, often resulting in malnutrition and starvation.

**guerrillas**  Small fighting forces of volunteer soldiers, often engaging in surprise attacks against much larger, better-organized government troops.

**ideology**  The group of ideas upon which a particular theory, philosophy, or economic or political system is based.

**intellectual**  Someone engaged in educational pursuits; activities relating to the mind and its enrichment; someone from the educated class.

**malaria**  A disease caused by a parasite that is transmitted by the bite of infected mosquitoes.

**militia**  An army of citizens, rather than professional soldiers, often formed in times of national emergency.

**monarchy**  A system of government based upon the rule of a king or queen. The right to rule is passed down through the family, rather than through elections or appointments.

**monk**  A man who withdraws from society, gives up his possessions, accepts poverty, joins a religious order, and devotes himself to mostly solitary religious devotion.

**nationalist**  A member of a political party or group advocating national independence, autonomy, or strong national government.

**overlord**  A ruler or master.

**paranoia**  A mental disorder resulting in delusions, a sense of persecution, and constant suspiciousness.

**propaganda**  The systematic and widespread dissemination of ideas or doctrines to support one's cause or damage an opposing cause.

**refugee**  A person who flees his or her home or country to seek shelter elsewhere.

**sovereign**  Possessing independent authority.

**utopian**  Describes a visionary scheme for the perfect society; an idealized place, state, or situation.

# FOR MORE INFORMATION

Cambodian Genocide Group (CGG)
567 West 125th Street, Suite 3B
New York, NY 10021
(203) 809-7197
Web site: http://www.cambodiangenocide.org/front.htm
> CGG is an international nonprofit student organization that
> works with governments, nongovernmental organizations, and the
> Cambodian people to further the process of truth and reconciliation.
> It also increases awareness and supports initiatives that prevent
> genocide and human rights violations from occurring.

The Cambodian Genocide Project, Inc.
Genocide Watch
P.O. Box 809
Washington, DC 20044
(703) 448-0222
Web site: http://www.genocidewatch.org/CambodianGenocideProject.htm
> This organization was founded in 1982 to bring the leaders of the
> Khmer Rouge regime in Democratic Kampuchea to justice. Since
> 1998, the Cambodian Genocide Project has been a division of
> Genocide Watch, the coordinator for the International Campaign to
> End Genocide.

Crimes of War Project
1325 G Street NW, Suite 730
Washington, DC 20005
(202) 638-0230
Web site: http://www.crimesofwar.org

The Crimes of War Project is a collaboration of journalists, lawyers, and scholars dedicated to raising public awareness of the laws of war and their application to situations of conflict.

The Dith Pran Holocaust Awareness Project, Inc.
P.O. Box 1616
Woodbridge, NJ 07095
Web site: http://www.dithpran.org
   The project was founded by Dith Pran, a Cambodian refugee whose wartime story was portrayed in the movie *The Killing Fields*. Dith Pran and Kim DePaul, executive director of the project, aim to continue to educate American students about the Cambodian genocide.

Office of the United Nations High Commissioner
   for Human Rights (OHCHR)
Palais des Nations
CH-1211 Geneva 10
Switzerland
Web site: http://www.ohchr.org
   OHCHR is the principal United Nations office mandated to protect and promote human rights for all people.

United Human Rights Council (UHRC)
P.O. Box 10039
Glendale, CA 91206
Web site: http://www.unitedhumanrights.org
   UHRC seeks to call attention to those governments that distort, deny, and revise their own history to disguise past and present genocides, massacres, and human rights violations. UHRC campaigns include education, awareness, political activism, petition drives, and consumer boycotts.

Yale University's Cambodian Genocide Program
P.O. Box 208206
New Haven, CT 06520-8206
Web site: http://www.yale.edu/cgp/index.html
   Since 1994, this award-winning program, a project of the Genocide
   Studies Program at Yale University's MacMillan Center for Inter-
   national and Area Studies, has been studying to learn as much as
   possible about the Cambodian tragedy and to help determine who
   was responsible for the crimes of the Pol Pot regime.

## WEB SITES

Due to the changing nature of Internet links, Rosen Publishing has
developed an online list of Web sites related to the subject of this book.
This site is updated regularly. Please use this link to access the list:

http://www.rosenlinks.com/gmt/krcg

# FOR FURTHER READING

Allen, John. *Pol Pot* (History's Villains). Farmington Hills, MI: Blackbirch Press, 2005.

Brown, Ian. *Cambodia: The Background, the Issues, the People* (Oxfam Country Profile). Oxford, England: Oxfam Publishing, 2000.

Des Chenes, Elizabeth, ed. *Genocide* (Contemporary Issues Companion). Farmington Hills, MI: Greenhaven, 2007.

January, Brendan. *Genocide: Modern Crimes Against Humanity*. Minneapolis, MN: Twenty-First Century Books, 2007.

Koopmans, Andy. *Pol Pot* (Heroes and Villains). Farmington Hills, MI: Lucent Books, 2005.

Kras, Sara Louise. *Cambodia: Enchantment of the World*. New York, NY: Children's Press, 2005.

Sheehan, Sean, and Barbara Cooke. *Cambodia* (Cultures of the World). New York, NY: Benchmark Books, 2007.

Spangeburg, Ray, and Kit Moser. *The Crime of Genocide: Terror Against Humanity* (Issues in Focus). Berkeley Heights, NJ: Enslow Publishers, 2000.

Springer, Jane. *Genocide* (Groundwork Guides). Toronto, ON: Groundwood Books, 2007.

# BIBLIOGRAPHY

Chandler, David P. *Brother Number One: A Political Biography of Pol Pot.* Boulder, CO: Westview Press, 1999.

Chandler, David. *Voices from S-21: Terror and History in Pol Pot's Secret Prison.* Berkeley, CA: University of California Press, 1999.

DePaul, Kim, ed. *Children of Cambodia's Killing Fields: Memoirs by Survivors.* New Haven, CT: Yale University Press, 1997.

Fuller, Thomas. "Couple Who Helped Lead Khmer Rouge Are Arrested." *New York Times.* November 13, 2007. Retrieved November 2007 (http://www.nytimes.com/2007/11/13/world/asia/13cambo.html).

Kiernan, Ben. *How Pol Pot Came to Power: Colonialism, Nationalism, and Communism in Cambodia, 1930–1975.* 2nd ed. New Haven, CT: Yale University Press, 2004.

Kiernan, Ben. *The Pol Pot Regime: Race, Power, and Genocide in Cambodia Under the Khmer Rouge, 1975–79.* 2nd ed. New Haven, CT: Yale University Press, 2002.

Mydans, Seth. "Former Khmer Rouge Leader Arrested." *New York Times.* September 20, 2007. Retrieved October 2007 (http://www.nytimes.com/2007/09/20/world/asia/20cambodia.html).

Mydans, Seth. "Out from Behind a Camera at a Khmer Torture House." *New York Times.* October 27, 2007. Retrieved October 2007 (http://query.nytimes.com/gst/fullpage.html?res=9805E1DA1231F934A15753C1A9619C8B63).

Richburg, Keith B. "Khmer Rouge Head Pol Pot Dies in Cambodia at Age 73." *The Tech* (MIT). April 17, 1998. Retrieved November 2007 (http://www-tech.mit.edu/V118/N20/akhmer.20w.html).

Short, Philip. *Pol Pot: Anatomy of a Nightmare.* New York, NY: Henry Holt and Company, LLC, 2004.

# INDEX

## ABOUT THE AUTHOR

Sean Bergin is a writer living in New York City who has written several books on government, politics, world leaders, and history. He has a master's degree in medieval literature, specializing in medieval Irish poetry. Through his study of Irish history, he has become keenly interested in other nations' experiences of colonialism and violent ethnic repression.

## PHOTO CREDITS

Cover (top), pp. 4 (left), 8, 14, 21, 29, 40 Manuel Ceneta/AFP/Getty Images; cover (bottom), pp. 9, 44, 50 Tang Chhin Sothy/AFP/Getty Images; pp. 4–5, 16 Jehangir Gazdar/Woodfin Camp/Time & Life Pictures/Getty Images; p. 10 LL/Roger Viollet/Getty Images; pp. 12, 13, 30, 41 AFP/Getty Images; pp. 15, 19, 26 © AP Images; p. 18 Thomas D. McAvoy/Time & Life Pictures/Getty Images; p. 23 William Lovelace/Hulton Archive/Getty Images; p. 24 Ian Brodie/Hulton Archive/Getty Images; p. 25 © Bettmann/Corbis; p. 27 Sjoberg/AFP/Getty Images; p. 32 © Richard Dudman/Sygma/Corbis; p. 33 John Bryson/Time & Life Pictures/Getty Images; p. 37 Francoise De Mulder/Roger Viollet/Getty Images; p. 39 Wilbur E. Garrett/National Geographic/Getty Images; p. 42 Alex Bowie/Hulton Archive/Getty Images; p. 46 Romeo Gacad/AFP/Getty Images; p. 48 Prasit Sangrungrueng/AFP/Getty Images.

Designer: Tahara Anderson; Photo Researcher: Cindy Reiman